Structural Wonders

Pyramids of Giza

Sheelagh Matthews

Weigl Publishers Inc.

Published by Weigl Publishers Inc.
350 5th Avenue, Suite 3304, PMB 6G
New York, NY 10118-0069

Website: www.weigl.com

Copyright ©2008 WEIGL PUBLISHERS INC.
All rights reserved. No part of this publication may be reproduced, stored
in a retrievalsystem, or transmitted in any form or by any means, electronic,
mechanical, photocopying, recording, or otherwise, without the prior written
permission of Weigl Publishers Inc.

Library of Congress Cataloging-in-Publication Data

Matthews, Sheelagh.
  Pyramids of Giza / Sheelagh Matthews.
      p. cm. -- (Structural wonders)
  Includes index.
  ISBN 978-1-59036-725-4 (hard cover : alk. paper) -- ISBN 978-1-59036-726-1 (soft cover :
alk. paper)
  1. Pyramids of Giza (Egypt)--Juvenile literature. 2. Pyramids of Giza (Egypt)--Design and
construction--Juvenile literature. I. Title.
  DT63.M32 2007
  932--dc22
                                    2007012123

Printed in the United States of America
1 2 3 4 5 6 7 8 9 0 11 10 09 08 07

Photograph Credits
Every reasonable effort has been made to trace ownership and to obtain
permission to reprint copyright material. The publishers would be pleased
to have any errors or omissions brought to their attention so that they may
be corrected in subsequent printings.

All of the internet URLs given in the book were valid at the time of publication.
However, due to the dynamic nature of the Internet, some addresses may have
changed, or sites may have ceased to exist since publication. While the author
and publisher regret any inconvenience this may cause readers, no responsibility
for any such changes can be accepted by either the author or the publisher.

Project Coordinators: Heather C. Hudak, Heather Kissock
Design: Terry Paulhus

Contents

What are the Pyramids of Giza?

Humans have been building ever since they could use tools. The techniques and materials may have changed over the ages, but building structures of all kinds continues to this day. Houses, office buildings, churches, towers, and monuments are all structures.

Some structures, such as the Pyramids of Giza, are known throughout the world. The pyramids were built by a civilization that lived almost 4,500 years ago. They were built on a strong rock **plateau** called the Giza Plateau, a few miles south of Cairo, the capital of Egypt.

The Pyramids of Giza consist of three pyramid complexes built as tombs for Egyptian kings. The three pyramids at Giza were built over three generations and 100 years. The oldest and largest of the three main pyramids is known as the Great Pyramid. It is the world's largest pyramid and the only one of the **Seven Wonders of the Ancient World** that remains today.

The two smaller main pyramids are known as the Pyramid of Kafre and the Pyramid of Menkaure. They are named after the people for whom they were built. The Sphinx stands watch over the Pyramids of Giza. This structure has the head of a king and the body of a lion. In addition, there are several other structures, including three smaller pyramids, a boat pit, and several temples and **mastabas**.

Quick Bites

- In Arabic, the Sphinx's name is *Abu al-Hol*, which means "Father of Terror." The Greeks gave the structure the name *Sphinx*, after a mythical creature.
- After an earthquake in the 14th century, the Pyramids of Giza were looted by robbers. Ancient treasures, such as paintings, sculptures, pottery, weapons, jewelry, and other personal belongings, were stolen. Even the Great Pyramid's **capstone**, which was likely covered in gold, was removed.

Building History

Egypt is a very old civilization. Its history is divided into several periods, generally following the rule of 30 dynasties. A dynasty is a series of rulers from the same royal family. The greatest of these periods are the Old Kingdom (2700–2200 BC), Middle Kingdom (2050–1800 BC), and New Kingdom (1550–1070 BC). The Pyramid Age belongs to Egypt's Old Kingdom, but kings of the Old, Middle, and New Kingdoms were all buried in pyramids.

Construction of the very first pyramid was started around 2630 BC by King Djoser. He was the second king of the Old Kingdom. A towering stepped stone structure was constructed for his tomb at Saqqara, about 12 miles (19 kilometers) south of present-day Cairo. It became known as the Step Pyramid of Djoser. This 204-foot (61-meter) tall structure was visible for miles in the desert. It inspired later kings to build similar structures.

At 204 feet (62 m), the Step Pyramid of Djoser was the largest building at the time.

Many artifacts have been uncovered in Saqqara, including tombs of nobles, a seated statue of King Djoser, and wall murals.

Khafre ruled from 2520–2494 BC. He built the second-largest pyramid.

In 2613 BC, about 35 years after King Djoser died, King Sneferu took over Egypt's throne. King Sneferu sought perfection in pyramid construction. Although he needed only one burial place, King Sneferu worked on three large structures in his quest for a perfectly smooth-faced pyramid.

Heiroglyphics have been found from the Pyramid of Teti, the first king of Egypt's sixth dynasty.

The Pyramids of Giza and the Sphinx were built at the height of the Pyramid Age, about 4,500 years ago. Sneferu's son and successor, King Khufu, built the Great Pyramid at Giza.

King Khufu's successors—his son, Khafre, and his grandson, Menkaure—built the remaining two main pyramids at Giza. They were built mostly out of granite and limestone. Polished white limestone surrounded the pyramids, making them shine brightly in the desert sun. It is believed that Khafre also built the Sphinx at Giza.

The Pyramids of Giza are an imposing sight on the Egyptian desert.

Big Ideas

The kings of Egypt were considered gods on Earth. These gods were called "kings" during the time of the Old Kingdom. Later, after 1450 BC, they were known as "pharaohs." Whether kings or pharaohs, Egypt's rulers were honored as gods in both life and death.

After death, ancient Egyptians believed their kings went to live with the gods in the Kingdom of Osiris. Osiris was the god of the Underworld. It was believed that a pyramid, a structure that pointed to the stars in the heavens, could help a king's spirit rise to the Kingdom of Osiris. Pyramids were aligned with the stars in **Orion's constellation**, as these stars were believed to house Osiris's soul.

As pyramids took a long time to build, the first duty of an Egyptian king was to start construction of his tomb. The tomb would house and care for a king's divine body in the **afterlife**. Bodies of kings were preserved as **mummies** and placed in their pyramids after death.

Ancient pyramids contained priceless jewelry, beautiful sculptures, and walls of hieroglyphic engravings and paintings. Pyramids housed many of the king's personal belongings, including weapons, for his use in the next world.

Web Link:
To find out more about ancient Egypt, go to www.mfa.org/egypt

1) Menkaure ruled between 2490 and 2472 BC. A statue of the king was found at Giza. 2) Excavations for treasures from ancient Egypt often take place at or near the Pyramids of Giza. 3) Queen Mereret's jewelry was found in her tomb at the Pyramids of Dashur.

Profile:
Imhotep and Ancient Egyptian Architects

Kings appointed their own royal architects to oversee the construction of their pyramid in ancient Eypt. The main architect of the Great Pyramid was Hemon, a relative of King Khufu.

Imhotep is considered to be the world's first architect. He is known as the designer of the first pyramid ever to be built, the Step Pyramid of Djoser, at Saqqara, Egypt. The inventor of stone construction, Imhotep is thought of as the first structural engineer. The same methods he developed are used in the construction of structures today.

The entrance to King Djoser's tomb is a great hall lined with large stone columns. Building with stone was new to the Egyptians. It is possible that Imhotep designed and built the first architectural columns known to humankind.

THE WORK OF THE ANCIENT EGYPTIANS

Luxor Temple

Located on the east banks of the Nile River, Luxor Temple was dedicated to the three most powerful Egyptian gods—Amun, Mut, and Khonsu. Amenophis III was the main architect for the temple, which included a causeway lined by sphinxes, a 79-foot (24 m) pylon, four large statues of Ramesses II, two pink granite obelisks, courtyards, and a temple. Today, only the ruins of this temple remain.

Nubian Monuments

Located on the western bank of Lake Nasser, this **UNESCO World Heritage Site** was built between 1284 and 1264 BC. The temple complex is known as the Temple of Ramesses, beloved by Amun, and it consists of two temples.

Ancient Egyptian architects used a standard unit of measure called a royal cubit, which is about 20 inches (51 centimeters). A cubit was about the length of a person's forearm. It was divided into smaller units by palms and fingers. Architects made mathematical calculations, using squares, circles, and triangles. They relied on the North Star and the study of angles to help with the alignment of the pyramids.

Accuracy in measuring and positioning was extremely important in pyramid building. The Great Pyramid is oriented to the four compass points—true north, south, east, and west. Astronomers helped with the orientation by aligning the Great Pyramid with the stars. Then, surveyors measured and leveled the site. If the alignment of the sides was wrong, they would not meet at the top.

The Step Pyramid is considered to be the first Egyptian tomb made entirely of stone.

King Tutankhamun's Tomb

King Tut's tomb was found almost completely intact in 1922. Compared to other ancient Egyptian kings, the tomb is small, consisting of a passage that leads to four simple chambers.

Hatshepsut's Temple

Located in Deir el-Bahri, this structure was designed by Senenmut, the royal architect. The temple was to be used to worship Queen Hatshepsut after her death. A ramp leads to a series of colonnaded terraces that were once lined with gardens. Most of the statues and ornaments of this temple are now missing.

The Science Behind the Building

Building any structure requires planning, physical labor, and technology. The people who built the pyramids had to use their knowledge of scientific principles to ensure that the structures were strong and durable.

Geometry and Triangles

In ancient Egypt, basic **geometrical** figures were used to build the pyramids. A pyramid has four equal triangular sides that meet in a point. The base of a pyramid is a square.

Triangles are basic parts of geometry. They are the strongest and most stable shapes known to humans. Unlike a four-sided frame, a triangle shape will not collapse, or fail. For example, if force is applied the corner of a square, the square becomes a diamond shape. If force is applied to the corner of a triangle, its shape stays the same.

Triangles help strengthen many structures. They are often found in bridges, hydro towers, railway trestles, **geodesic domes**, and skyscrapers. The pyramids were constructed using equal-sized triangles, each supporting the other as they rose to a point at the top.

Engineers calculate the "live load" of a building, which includes the weight of people and objects in the building.

Withstanding Weight

The Pyramids of Giza were built on a solid stone plateau that could support their heavy load. Loads are forces that act on structures, such as weight, wind, temperature, or vibration. The weight of any structure itself is called a "dead load."

The Giza Plateau was made of very hard stone. This high, flat, and hard area made an excellent construction site. A soft surface, like the desert sand, would not be strong enough to support the Pyramids of Giza. The pyramids would experience "settlement load" on a soft surface. This means they would have sunk and possibly changed shape if built on sand.

The Properties of Stone

Natural stone is one of the oldest building materials known to humans. Structures made of stone will last a long time. Most stone is weather resistant, will not catch fire, and will not soften if it comes in contact with water. When temperature causes a structure to change shape, it is called the "thermal load." Stone is not sensitive to temperature changes. It does not expand much when it becomes hot and does not shrink much when it cools. The pyramids were built in a desert region, with hot sun during the day and cold nights. Stone was a good choice of construction material for the pyramids in these wide-ranging temperature conditions.

Web Link:
To find out more about geometry, visit www.scienceu.com/geometry

Science and Technology

The ancient Egyptians constructed the massive pyramids without the help of machines or power tools. However, they used innovative technology and hand tools to ease their workload.

To build the pyramids, the Egyptians needed large amounts of stone. Local quarries supplied most of the core stones used in the pyramids. The fine limestone used for the Great Pyramid's shining outer casing came from Turah.

Sleds

Granite is a much harder rock than limestone. King Khufu's burial chambers were lined with granite. Granite quarries were almost 580 miles (934 km) away from the Great Pyramid's site. Granite had to be moved to the pyramid site along the Nile River. It is believed that the pyramid's large stone blocks were transported over land using wooden sleds called sledges. Using ropes, teams of 20 men pulled the heavy sleds across wooden tracks. Other laborers poured water over these wooden tracks. Wetting the tracks made it easier for the sleds to slide.

Levers help to lift and dig. Many tools, including shovels, operate as levers.

Levers

Putting the capstone on the pyramid was difficult and dangerous. There was not much room at the top of the pyramid for workers to move the capstone into place. Long wooden levers were needed to help take the place of men. A lever is like an arm that pivots, or turns, against a **fulcrum**. In general, the longer the arm of the lever, the easier it is to perform the work of prying objects apart. For example, the long arm of a shovel makes it easier to pull out the long roots of a stubborn weed than weeding by hand. In this example, the shovel acts as a lever, and the soil acts as the fulcrum.

Ramps are useful in today's world as well. Vehicles can be driven up a ramp to get to a higher place. They do not have to be lifted.

Ramps

Ramps are inclined planes. An inclined plan is a flat surface that is slanted. Inclined planes allow things to be moved with less effort. The ancient Egyptians did not have mechanical cranes to lift a pyramid's heavy stone blocks into place. Instead, they may have dragged the stone blocks up to the pyramid using ramps. Some historians believe that one long ramp was used. As the pyramid got higher, the ramp got longer. This made sure the ramp was never too steep. Other historians believe that ramps went around the pyramid. Ramps were made using mud, stone, and wood.

Wedges

Stone-cutting tools were used to cut a pyramid's massive stone blocks from the quarry. Many of these tools were wedges. Wedges use the pointed end of an inclined plane to do work. A wedge pushes things apart by converting motion on one direction into a splitting motion at the other end. The splitting occurs at right angles to the pointed part of the wedge. The handheld wedges used to cut the stone for the pyramids were made out of a type of stone that was harder than the stone being quarried for the pyramid. This allowed the wedges to cut into the rock without breaking. Limestone was quarried by channeling around blocks of stone. The channels had to be at least as wide as one person. This allowed room for a worker to cut away at the rock with a pick. It is believed that blocks of granite were also channeled out, like limestone blocks. Workers used hand-held pounders made of dolerite to cut channels into granite.

Quick Bites

- Before the first pyramid was built, tombs for kings were large structures, but much lower in height. They were mastabas constructed of mud brick, instead of stone.
- There are many theories about the power of pyramids. One suggests that pyramids were places that could be used to predict the future. Some people claim that knives are sharper and foods are improved when stored in a pyramid.

Computer-Aided Design

Architects are trained professionals who work with clients to design structures. Before anything is built, they make detailed drawings or models. These plans are important tools that help people visualize what the structure will look like. A blueprint is a detailed diagram that shows where all the parts of the structure will be placed. Walls, doors, windows, plumbing, electrical wiring, and other details are mapped out on the blueprint. Blueprints act as a guide for engineers and builders during construction.

For centuries, architects and builders worked without the aid of computers. Sketches and blueprints were drawn by hand. Highly skilled drafters would draw very technical designs. Today, this process is done using computers and sophisticated software programs. Architects use CAD, or computer-aided design, throughout the design process. Early CAD systems used computers to draft building plans. Today's computer programs can do much more. They can build three-dimensional models and computer simulations of how a building will look. They can also calculate the effects of different physical forces on the structure. Using CAD, today's architects can build more complex structures at lower cost and in less time.

Computer-aided design programs have been used since the 1960s.

Eye on Design

Three-Dimensional Tools Recreate Pyramid Construction

For centuries, people have tried to determine how the ancient Egyptians constructed the massive pyramids.

New technology created by Dassault Systemes has provided a detailed analysis on what may have happened 4,500 years ago.

Using a three-dimensional software application, a team of scientists reconstructed the site of the Great Pyramid and tested a number of construction theories developed by author and architect Jean-Pierre Houdin. They wanted to know how laborers hoisted materials to the top of the pyramid. Through a series of mathematical calculations, the team tried to determine if one large ramp, levers and wedges, or a spiral ramp was used.

By reconstructing the building site, the team was able to confirm that laborers likely used a ramp to carry material 141 feet (43 m) up the pyramid. Another ramp was built inside the pyramid to carry materials above that height. A carriage on a bed of wooden rollers hauled items to the top of the structure.

Location

The Pyramids of Giza are located on the Giza Plateau in Egypt. The plateau is situated on the west bank of the Nile River and is bordered by the city of Giza and the Sahara Desert.

Height

- The Great Pyramid stands 481 feet (146.5 m) high. It is as tall as a 48-story skyscraper and was the tallest standing structure in the world for 4,300 years.

- The Pyramid of Khafre stands 471 feet (143.5 m) high.

- The Pyramid of Menkaure stands 226 feet (68.8 m) high.

Base

- Each side of the square base of the Great Pyramid is about 755 feet (230 m) long. The area of the Great Pyramid's base covers just over 13 acres (5.3 hectares).

- Each side of the square base of the Pyramid of Khafre is about 704 feet (214.5 m) long.

- Each side of the square base of the Pyramid of Menkaure is about 345.5 feet (105 m) long.

Weight

The Great Pyramid is made with almost 2.3 million blocks of stone. On average, each stone weighs about 2.5 tons (2.2 tonnes).

Other Interesting Facts

- The Great Pyramid is the only pyramid to have chambers above ground level.

Slope

Each triangular side of the Great Pyramid sits at a slope of about 51 degrees.

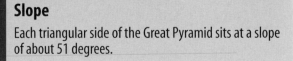

Environmental Viewpoint

The physical environment can have a big affect on a structure. Built in the desert, the Pyramids of Giza have withstood several forces of nature, from winds and floods to earthquakes.

There were many advantages to choosing the Giza Plateau to construct the pyramids. As these monuments are extremely heavy, they need a strong base, or foundation, on which to rest. The hard stone plateau provides a surface strong enough to withstand the enormous weight of the pyramids. The plateau was also high enough to keep the pyramids out of water during the Nile River's annual flood.

Windstorms and sandstorms are common in the desert. Weathering occurs when rock is weakened or decayed by natural elements. The desert's hot sun and blowing sand weathers the pyramid's stone blocks. Then, the wind strips small particles of stone from the pyramid's walls. This is called erosion. For the most part, the Pyramids of Giza have withstood the sandblasting effect of desert winds for thousands of years.

The high volume of tourist traffic to the area is having an adverse effect on the pyramids and their surrounding environment.

In addition to natural weathering, the pyramids face damage from humans who visit the site. Garbage, such as pop cans, litter the area. At one time, people were allowed to climb to the top of the pyramids. Although this is no longer allowed, some people still attempt to scale the sides of the crumbling structures. Many of those who have made it to the top have etched their names in the stone.

POTENTIAL PROBLEMS

The Pyramids of Giza have been amazing tourist attractions since ancient times. The Giza Plateau now borders the city of Giza, a large urban area. Being close to an airport and hotels helps give rise to a strong tourism industry in the area.

Many visitors travel from all parts of the world each year to see and experience the Pyramids of Giza. Due to the high volume of tourists, however, there is a greater chance of damage to the pyramids and their surroundings.

To help combat these potential problems, the Pyramids of Giza have been named a UNESCO World Heritage Site. A World Heritage Site is for all people of the world to enjoy. UNESCO provides technical assistance and professional training to help protect World Heritage Sites. This helps protect and conserve the pyramids from urban and tourism development. It helps discourage tourists from removing pieces of stone or other souvenirs from the site.

Construction Careers

It took almost 20,000 to 30,000 men about 20 years to build the Great Pyramid. Workers included laborers, metalworkers, stonemasons, water carriers, carpenters, painters, and sculptors. **Scribes** kept track of all the materials needed. They wrote in hieroglyphics using **papyrus** and pens made out of reeds. Artists painted walls and sculpted statues. Craftspeople made pottery, jewelry, and weapons for the king to use in the afterlife. In addition, men worked on ships to help transport supplies and stone blocks from the quarry.

Stonemasons

Stonemasons were responsible for cutting the core blocks for the pyramids and shaping the stone. After the ramps were removed from the pyramids and the construction materials were cleared away, stonemasons began working on the surface of the structures. They would smooth and polish the rock to give it a refined finish. Today, masons continue to work on buildings. They shape bricks and stones and lay them in place.

Laborers

Laborers made up the majority of workers on the Pyramids of Giza. Many laborers were farmers who built the pyramids when they were not working the land. Laborers were responsible for doing many tasks. They lifted heavy rocks, prepared meals, and carried water. Laborers continue to play an important role in construction. They perform many jobs, including cleaning sites, building concrete forms, loading materials, and operating equipment. Some jobs require special training, while others can be done without experience. However, laborers should be physically fit to do most jobs.

Carpenters

Carpenters played an important role in the construction of the pyramids. They made tools that were used by other trades. Carpenters carved wooden statues and adornments for the inside the pyramids. These workers are important to construction today. They perform many different woodworking tasks. Some carpenters build the frames for buildings, such as houses. Other carpenters make furniture. Carpentry is often done outdoors, especially on buildings. Most carpenters learn the trade by working with others who are skilled at the craft.

Web Link:
To find out more about carpenters, visit www.bls.gov/oco/ocos202.htm

Notable Structures

Different types of pyramids are found all around the world. Other cultures built pyramids as temples or capitals of empires instead of tombs. Not all pyramids from other cultures are made of stone. Some were made of mud and brick, others with glass and steel.

Etemenanki

Rebuilt: 625–539 BC

Location: Babylon, ancient Mesopotamia

Design: Sumerians

Description: Etemenanki was a seven-story **ziggurat** that was dedicated to a god named Marduk. Today, little remains of the structure that likely inspired Biblical stories of the Tower of Babel.

Templo Mayor (Great Pyramid Temple)

Built: Around 1390 AD

Location: Mexico City, Mexico

Design: Aztecs

Description: This stepped pyramid was built as a temple to two Aztec gods. Templo Mayor was mostly destroyed in 1521, when the Aztecs were conquered by Spain.

Today's modern architects use the pyramid form to construct office buildings, museums, and monuments. Small pyramids cap the tops of obelisks.

Canary Wharf Tower

Built: 1991

Location: London, England

Design: Cesar Pelli, architect

Description: At 800 feet (235 m) high, this 50-story skyscraper is capped with a pyramid, making the structure look like a giant obelisk. It houses 6.6 million square feet (613,000 sq m) of office space.

Transamerica Pyramid

Built: 1970

Location: San Francisco, California

Design: William L. Pereira & Associates, architects

Description: Transamerica Insurance & Investment Group built this landmark office building. It is 48 stories high, with 530,000 square feet (49,239 sq m) of space. Its largest floor measures 145 feet (44 m) per side. Its smallest floor measures only 45 feet (14 m) per side.

Pyramids Around the World

Pyramids have been built all around the world. Some were built by ancient civilizations, such as the Egyptians. Others were built in the past several decades.

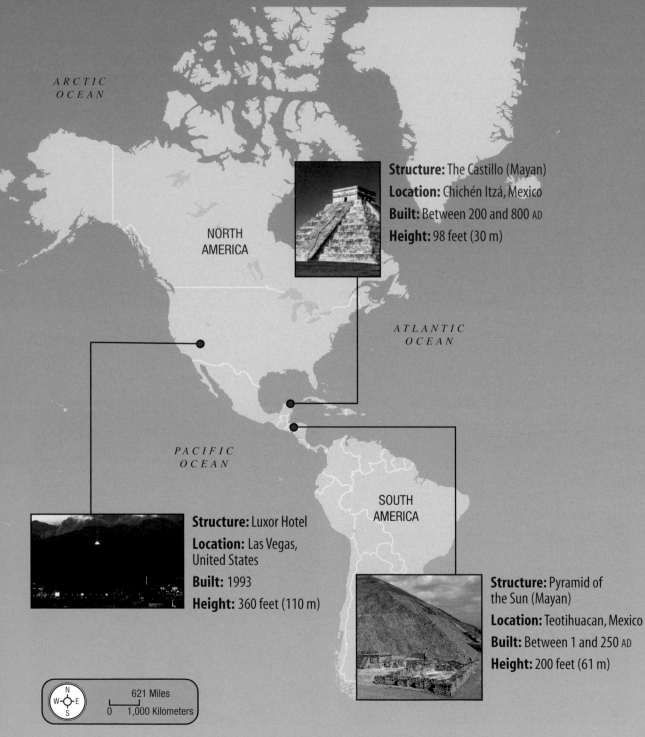

Structure: The Castillo (Mayan)
Location: Chichén Itzá, Mexico
Built: Between 200 and 800 AD
Height: 98 feet (30 m)

Structure: Luxor Hotel
Location: Las Vegas, United States
Built: 1993
Height: 360 feet (110 m)

Structure: Pyramid of the Sun (Mayan)
Location: Teotihuacan, Mexico
Built: Between 1 and 250 AD
Height: 200 feet (61 m)

ARCTIC OCEAN

NORTH AMERICA

ATLANTIC OCEAN

PACIFIC OCEAN

SOUTH AMERICA

621 Miles
0   1,000 Kilometers

Throughout the continents, examples of pyramids have been used as monuments, temples, displays of artwork, and places of business. This map shows a few examples of pyramids.

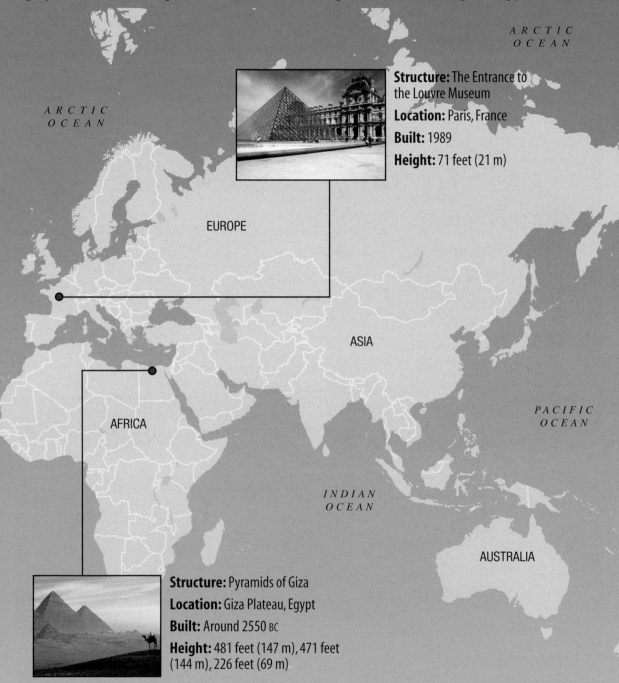

Structure: The Entrance to the Louvre Museum

Location: Paris, France

Built: 1989

Height: 71 feet (21 m)

Structure: Pyramids of Giza

Location: Giza Plateau, Egypt

Built: Around 2550 BC

Height: 481 feet (147 m), 471 feet (144 m), 226 feet (69 m)

Quiz

Q Who was responsible for the first pyramid ever built?

A King Djoser ordered the construction of the first pyramid. Imhotep was the architect.

Q What are the characteristics of a pyramid?

A A pyramid has four equal triangular sides that rise to a point. The base of a pyramid is a square.

Q How was the Great Pyramid positioned on the landscape?

A Astronomers aligned the Great Pyramid with the stars in the night sky. Then, surveyors measured and leveled the site. If the sides were not aligned correctly, the sides would not meet at the top.

Q What are loads?

A Loads are forces, such as weight, wind, temperature, and vibrations, that act on structures.

Build a Gumdrop Dome

Triangles are the most stable building unit. One of the strongest building structures, made entirely of triangles, is known as a geodesic dome. Each triangle is connected to another one. These shapes form a rigid, but spherical framework, creating a dome. Each side of every triangle shares the load of the weight of this building equally.

Geodesic domes are strong, lightweight, and easy to construct. Try building a small-scale geodesic dome out of gumdrops and toothpicks.

Materials
- 11 gumdrops
- 25 toothpicks that are pointed at both ends

Instructions

1. Use gumdrops to connect five toothpicks in a ring. This will result in a base that is in the shape of a pentagon.

2. Use two toothpicks and one gumdrop to make a triangle on one side of this base.

3. Repeat, making triangles all around the pentagon-shaped base.

4. Use toothpicks to connect the gumdrops at the tops of the triangles. How many triangles do you have?

5. Push one toothpick into each of the top gumdrops.

6. Use the last gumdrop to connect these toothpicks at the top.

7. Try testing the dome's strength by pressing down on one point of its many triangles. What does it do?

8. Using extra gumdrops and toothpicks, make a box. Press down on one of the points of the box. What does it do? How does this compare to the triangle?

Further Research

You can find more information on the Pyramids of Giza, Ancient Egypt, and the world's best-known structures at your local library or on the Internet.

Websites

For more information about pyramids, visit
www.pbs.org/wgbh/nova/pyramid

Learn more about ancient Egypt at
www.nationalgeographic.com/pyramids/pyramids.html

Find out about the construction of Egypt's pyramids at
www.history.com/minisites/diggingforthetruth

Glossary

afterlife: the time after a person's death

capstone: the top stone on a structure

fulcrum: the pivot around which a lever turns

geodesic domes: light, structural frameworks arranged as a set of polygons in the form of a shell

geometrical: concerned with a branch of mathematics that deals with measurement

hieroglyphic: relating to an ancient Egyptian language using symbols for words and numbers

mastabas: flat-roofed, rectangular mud-brick buildings found above underground burial chambers; from the Arabic word for bench, as these structures have a similar shape to a bench

mummies: preserved bodies wrapped in strips of linen

obelisk: a tall square-shaped tower capped by the shape of a pyramid

Orion's constellation: a group of stars that form a specific design

papyrus: Egyptian paper made out of reeds

plateau: flat and table-like land, usually higher than the land around it

scribes: ancient Egyptians who could read and write

Seven Wonders of the Ancient World: the seven structures considered by scholars to be the most wondrous of the ancient world

UNESCO World Heritage Site: a place designated by the United Nations Educational, Scientific and Cultural Organization to be of cultural significance to the world and in need of protection

ziggurat: a form of temple tower built in Mesopotamia, somewhat like a stepped pyramid with a flat top

Index